Anya Gupta

The Kind Kitchen

PLANT-BASED VITILIGO TRANSFORMATION

NewDelhi • London

BLUEROSE PUBLISHERS
India | U.K.

Copyright © Anya Gupta 2024

All rights reserved by the author. No part of this publication may be reproduced, stored in a retrieval system or transmitted in any form or by any means, electronic, mechanical, photocopying, recording or otherwise, without the prior permission of the author. Although every precaution has been taken to verify the accuracy of the information contained herein, the publisher assumes no responsibility for any errors or omissions. No liability is assumed for damages that may result from the use of information contained within.

BlueRose Publishers takes no responsibility for any damages, losses, or liabilities that may arise from the use or misuse of the information, products, or services provided in this publication.

For permissions requests or inquiries regarding this publication,
please contact:

BLUEROSE PUBLISHERS
www.BlueRoseONE.com
info@bluerosepublishers.com
+91 8882 898 898
+4407342408967

ISBN: 978-93-5989-903-9

Cover design: Rishav
Typesetting: Rohit

First Edition: August 2024

ACKNOWLEDGMENT

Profound gratitude, I extend my heartfelt appreciation to all those who have played an integral role in bringing this cookbook to fruition.

Without your unwavering love, support, and constant encouragement, I would not be here today, proudly sharing my transformative journey with each and every one of you.

Foremost among them are my beloved parents, who have steadfastly believed in me from the very beginning. Their unyielding faith in my potential has been a driving force behind my pursuit of this dream.

To my Dada and Dadi, whose boundless affection and care have enveloped me like a warm embrace, I owe immeasurable gratitude for teaching me the essence of unconditional love.

I want to extend a special thank you to Ipsita for her remarkable design skills, which have breathed life into these pages and made this book so exquisite.

And to my mentor, Shruti Sharma, you have been my guiding light. With infinite patience, boundless support, and an abundance of love, you have helped me through the challenges of these last few months, nurturing my growth and refining my vision.

Finally, my appreciation extends to each and every reader who takes hold of this cookbook, embracing its message with an open heart. May the flavors within these recipes evoke joy and healing in your lives, and may my story serve as a reminder that each of us possesses a unique and undeniable beauty that deserves to be cherished.

With utmost sincerity and grace.

Anya Gupta

AUTHOR'S NOTE

Little did I know that Vitiligo would become an uninvited companion on my life's journey, shaping my experiences in ways I could never have anticipated. Growing up, I faced a constant battle for self-identity, a struggle that cast a shadow over the simplest joys of childhood. As the mirror was my biggest foe reflecting the physical differences that set me apart, and also echoing the emotional turmoil from within.

The journey from that vulnerable child to the person typing these words today has been a story of complete metamorphosis, one marked by resilience and growth. I chose not to let vitiligo script my entire narrative; instead, I embarked on a quest to reclaim my sense of self. This endeavor wasn't without its trials, and the path was far from linear. There were days when the weight of self-consciousness felt insurmountable, and nights when tears were shed both loudly and in private.

Amidst the struggle, a shift occurred. I decided that vitiligo wouldn't be the protagonist of my story; rather, it would be a footnote, a part of me but not the whole. This transformation didn't manifest overnight it was a gradual peeling away of the layers of shame and disgust. And in this process, I stumbled upon the beauty of self- acceptance and learned to treasure my uniqueness.

My exploration into controlling my auto-immune condition led me down numerous avenues, each one offering an individualistic glimmer of insight. Countless doctor visits later, I discovered an unexpected diet. This dietary change wasn't just about food; it was a complete lifestyle change. The path to this realization was laden with challenges, as I navigated the complexities of sustaining a vegan lifestyle while ensuring a balanced intake of vital nutrients. This cookbook stands as a testament to my determination to spare others the arduous trial-and-error journey I undertook. It wasn't a miraculous cure, but it was a source of hope. With each passing day on this new path, I witnessed my vitiligo patches receding like the tide, and with it, my fear of exposure diminished.

Today, I stand as a testament to the transformative power of embracing oneself fully. The decision to bare my skin to the world was both liberating and terrifying, a leap of faith that ultimately became a cornerstone of my personal growth. As I share this cookbook, a labor of love born from my own journey, I can't help but imagine the young souls who might find solace within its pages.

If a single person, staring at their reflection with uncertainty, can find a recipe that sparks a glimmer of self-assurance, then every moment of my struggle will have been worth it. This cookbook is more than a collection of recipes; it's a testament to human resilience, an embodiment of the warmth that comes from embracing imperfections. As I pour my heart into these words and recipes, I'm reminded of the vitality of the human spirit, capable of turning adversity into a catalyst for compassion and growth.

CONTENTS

Bean Bonanza Burger with a Twist 1

Exotic Vegan mac delight 3

Elegant Garden Medley with Creamy Cashew Dressing 6

Savory Basil-infused Baked Beans with Rice 8

Savory Zen Stir-Fried Medley 10

Velvet Peanut Butter Delight 13

Decadent Whole Wheat Vegan Fudge Brownies 16

Golden Vegan Banana Muffins 19

Silken Chocolate Delight 22

Cocoa-Hazelnut Spread 24

Creamy Green Delight: Avocado and Miso Dip 26

Eggplant Elegance: Refined Aubergine Delicacy 28

Savory Tofu Delight: Exquisite Sandwich Spread 30

Delicate Cashew Medley: A Refined Vegan Sandwich Spread 33

Savory Lentil Medley Bread 35

Sophisticated Gluten-Free Pizza Canvas 38

Gourmet Whole Wheat Pancakes 41

Whole Wheat Baguette Delight 43

Golden Garbanzo Brunch Delights 46

Vegan Tofu Cinnamon French Toast with Date Infusion 48

Golden Tofu Medley 51

Delicate Herb-infused Potato Galettes 53

Creamy Avocado Sunrise Bowl 56

Gourmet Delight Wrap 58

Basil-infused Tomato Bruschetta with Homemade Pesto 60

Gourmet Plant-Based Burger 63

Whole Wheat Blueberry Pancakes 65

Gourmet Herb-Roasted Potato Wedges 67

Nutty Date Granola Bars 69

Roasted Sweet Potato Delight 72

Bean Bonanza Burger with a Twist

Instructions:

1. In a mixing bowl, combine the cooked kidney beans, garam masala, chilli powder (if desired), cumin, minced onion, minced garlic, and homemade tomato ketchup.
2. Mash the mixture using a fork or potato masher until well combined, leaving some texture.
3. Gradually add the rolled oats to the mixture, stirring well to incorporate.
4. If the mixture appears dry, add coconut milk in small increments until a firm but moist consistency is achieved.
5. Shape the mixture into burger patties, ensuring they are compact and hold together.
6. Heat a non-stick pan or grill over medium heat and lightly grease with cooking spray or oil.
7. Cook the burger patties for approximately 4-5 minutes on each side, or until they develop a golden-brown crust and are heated through.
8. Remove the patties from the heat and let them rest for a few minutes before serving.
9. Serve the masala burgers on buns or lettuce wraps, accompanied by your choice of condiments and toppings.

Enjoy this delightful and flavorful burger as a nutritious and satisfying meal option!

INGREDIENTS

1 tsp minced onion

1 tsp minced garlic

⅓ cup rolled oats

½ tsp garam masala

3 tsp homemade tomato ketchup

¼ tsp chilli powder (optional)

4 tsp coconut milk (if needed)

½ tsp cumin

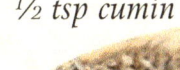

EXOTIC VEGAN MAC DELIGHT

Instructions:

1. Prepare the Vegetables:
- Clean and cut the carrot, green beans, capsicum, and onion into small, uniform pieces.

2. Cook the Macaroni:
- Fill a large pot with water and bring it to a boil.
- Add the macaroni noodles to the boiling water and cook according to the package instructions until al dente.
- Drain the cooked macaroni and toss it with 1 teaspoon of olive oil to prevent sticking. Set aside.

3. Steam the Vegetables:
- Steam the prepared vegetables until they are tender but still retain their crispness.
- Once cooked, set aside and allow them to cool.

4. Prepare the Sauce:
- In a wok or large pan, heat 2 and a half tablespoons of olive oil over medium heat.
- Add the minced garlic and sauté until fragrant.

5. Make the Roux:
- Sprinkle 1 tablespoon of white flour into the wok and stir continuously until it turns slightly brown.

6. Add the Coconut Milk:
   - Pour 100 ml of coconut milk and half a glass of water into the wok with the roux.
   - Stir well to combine and bring the mixture to a boil, creating a creamy sauce.
7. Incorporate the Vegetables and Pasta:
   - Add the steamed vegetables, cooked macaroni, and vegan cheese to the sauce.
   - Season with salt and pepper to taste.
   - Stir everything together, ensuring the cheese melts and coats the pasta and veggies.
   - Continue cooking for an additional 3-4 minutes until the flavors meld.
8. Alternative Baking Option:
   - Preheat the oven to 200 degrees Celsius.
   - Transfer the prepared pasta mixture to a baking dish.
   - Bake in the preheated oven for approximately 20 minutes, or until the top is golden and bubbly.

Serve this Exotic Vegan Mac Delight as a delightful vegan twist on the classic mac and cheese. Enjoy the creamy, flavorful combination of coconut milk, vegan cheese, and a medley of steamed vegetables. It's a wholesome and satisfying dish that will leave you wanting more!

INGREDIENTS

1 onion, finely chopped

Macaroni noodles

Salt and pepper to taste

Vegan cheese (with nutritional yeast)

2 & ½ tablespoons olive oil

A handful of green beans, trimmed and chopped

1 capsicum (bell pepper), diced

1 tablespoon white flour

Elegant Garden Medley with Creamy Cashew Dressing

Method:

1. In a large mixing bowl, combine the broccoli florets, sunflower seeds, chopped onion, and raisins. Toss gently to distribute the ingredients evenly.

2. In a blender, add the soaked and drained cashews, dates, apple cider vinegar, unrefined salt, and water. Blend on high speed until the mixture becomes smooth and creamy.

3. Pour the dressing over the salad ingredients in the mixing bowl. Use a spatula or large spoon to gently toss the salad, ensuring that all the ingredients are evenly coated with the dressing.

4. Serve immediately or refrigerate it for about 30 minutes to allow the flavors to meld together.

Note: This salad can be enjoyed as a refreshing side dish or a light meal on its own. The delightful combination of crunchy broccoli, nutty sunflower seeds, sweet raisins, and creamy dressing.

INGREDIENTS

½ cup cashews, soaked (4-6 hours) and drained

2 dates

¼ cup finely chopped red or sweet onion

6 tablespoons water

5 cups fresh broccoli florets

½ cup raisins

½ cup sunflower seeds

⅛ teaspoon unrefined salt

1 tablespoon apple cider vinegar

Savory Basil-Infused Baked Beans with Rice

Instructions:

1. Preheat the oven to 180°C (350°F).
2. In a pan, heat a little oil and fry the chopped onions until they turn golden brown.
3. Add the red pepper powder and chilli powder to the pan, stirring well to coat the onions evenly.
4. Drain the soaked brown rice and add it to the pan. Cook for 2-3 minutes, allowing the flavors to meld.
5. Add the tomatoes, black pepper, salt to taste, and 2 cups of water to the pan. Stir everything together and cook until the water is completely absorbed.
6. Take a large baking tray and spread the cooked beans evenly across the bottom.
7. Add the cooked rice on top of the beans and season with salt to your preference.
8. Sprinkle the chopped basil over the rice and beans mixture, ensuring even distribution.
9. Place the baking tray in the preheated oven and bake for approximately 40 minutes, or until the dish is heated through and the top layer turns golden.
10. Remove from the oven and let it cool slightly before serving.

Enjoy this delectable and nutritious baked beans with rice dish, perfectly infused with the aromatic flavors of basil.

INGREDIENTS

3 onions, finely chopped and lightly salted

Unrefined salt and freshly ground black pepper to taste

2/3 cup brown rice, washed and soaked for 8-10 hours

2 cups water

2 tomatoes, cut into small pieces

A handful of fresh basil, finely chopped

3 cups cooked beans

1 teaspoon chilli powder

Savory Zen Stir-Fried Medley

Method:

1. In a bowl, combine soy sauce, lemon juice, and grated ginger to create a marinade for the tofu.
2. Cut the tofu into ½ chunks and thoroughly coat them with the marinade. Allow the tofu to marinate for 45 minutes. Reserve the marinade.
3. Drain the tofu, ensuring to save the marinade. Heat a large pan and add the cauliflower, broccoli, carrots, onion, green pepper, and tofu. Stir the ingredients frequently to ensure even cooking.
4. Once the vegetables are slightly tender but still crunchy, add the snow peas, mushrooms, and green onions. Continue stirring frequently until the vegetables reach the desired texture.
5. Serve the stir-fried vegetables over cooked unpolished rice and drizzle with the reserved marinade.

Variations:

1. For an enhanced flavor profile, prepare the following ingredients before cooking the vegetables: finely chop or grate 5 cloves of garlic and an equal amount of peeled fresh ginger, keeping them separated. In a small pan, fry the garlic and ginger separately until browned. Store them together in a bowl. Spoon 1 tablespoon of date paste into the pan and cook for a minute. Add the fried ginger-garlic mixture, stir, and remove from heat. Sprinkle this mixture over the rice and vegetables.
2. For added texture and taste, consider topping the dish with roasted sesame seeds or roasted black sesame seeds.
3. Explore alternative vegetable options by stir-frying only Chinese greens and spinach, then topping them with the ginger-garlic mixture, sesame seeds, or both. Alternatively, incorporate different varieties of mushrooms for a unique twist on the recipe.

Enjoy the harmonious blend of flavors and textures in this delectable Savory Zen Stir-Fried Medley.

INGREDIENTS

2 cups cooked unpolished rice

1 cup cauliflower florets

pack tofu (100 – 150 g)

2 green spring onions, chopped

1 cup broccoli florets

1 medium onion, sliced

1 cup sliced mushrooms

¼ cup soy sauce

1/2 tsp grated fresh ginger root

¼ cup lemon juice

1 cup snow peas

green pepper, sliced

3 carrots, cut into 2" strips

Velvet Peanut Butter Delight

Method:

1. Begin by preparing a large strainer or colander. Line it with a fine cheesecloth, ensuring a smooth and refined presentation. Carefully pour the plain soy yogurt into the lined strainer, allowing any excess liquid to drain. Ensure the yogurt remains elevated above the collected liquid, maintaining its impeccable texture. Wrap the edges of the cheesecloth gently over the yogurt, enrobing it in an elegant embrace. Place the strainer or colander over a suitable pot, deep enough to capture the delicate liquid that escapes.

2. Preserve the integrity of the yogurt by preventing contact with the collected liquid. Securely cover the pot with a stretchy silicone cover or a layer of parchment paper, meticulously fastened with a delicate string. Allow this enchanting ensemble to reside within the cool confines of the refrigerator, a sanctuary of taste, for a minimum of 8 hours, so that the yogurt may acquire a sublime texture.

3. In a medium-sized bowl, harmoniously combine the strained yogurt, the luscious date paste, the pure vanilla extract, the smooth and velvety peanut butter, and a touch of unrefined salt. Unite these captivating ingredients with a gentle whisk until they meld into a symphony of flavors and textures, destined to enchant the palate.

4. The next step involves freezing this ethereal concoction within the embrace of an ice cream machine, adhering to the meticulous instructions bestowed by its revered manufacturer. As the freezing process nears completion, after approximately 5 minutes, grace this masterpiece with the finely chopped peanuts, introducing a delightful crunch and enhancing its regal essence.

5. For those who seek immediate gratification and an indulgence akin to a soft, heavenly cloud, savor this enchanting creation without delay. Serve promptly after freezing, luxuriating in its soft-serve consistency that is sure to captivate the senses.

6. For those desiring a firmer, more resolute experience reminiscent of traditional ice cream, carefully transfer this exquisite creation into an airtight container. Allow it to rest and develop its character within the cool embrace of the freezer for a minimum of 4 hours until it attains the desired level of firmness.

7. Prepare to be enthralled as you indulge in this Velvet Peanut Butter Delight, an irresistible fusion of sophisticated flavors and tantalizing textures. Let each spoonful transport you to a realm of refined decadence and blissful satisfaction.

INGREDIENTS

1 teaspoon of pure vanilla extract

½ cup of hand-selected peanuts, delicately chopped

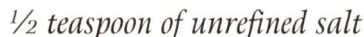

3 cups of premium plain soy yogurt

½ teaspoon of unrefined salt

½ cup of smooth, velvety peanut butter

Decadent Whole Wheat Vegan Fudge Brownies

Method:

1. Preheat the oven to 350 °F (180 °C).
2. In a large bowl, whisk together the whole wheat flour, cocoa powder, baking powder, baking soda, salt, walnuts, and chocolate chips (if using).
3. In a blender, combine the soy milk, date paste, tofu (or alternative), and vanilla extract. Blend until smooth and well incorporated.
4. Add the blended mixture to the flour mixture in the large bowl. Stir until just combined. The batter will be thick. If necessary, add a little extra soy milk to facilitate mixing.
5. Line an 8″ square baking dish with parchment paper. Spread the batter evenly into the dish.
6. Bake in the preheated oven for approximately 35 minutes, or until a toothpick inserted into the center comes out clean.
7. Remove from the oven and let cool completely in the baking dish.

8. Once cooled, carefully lift the brownies out of the dish using the parchment paper.
9. Cut into desired portions and serve.

Indulge in these rich and moist Whole Wheat Vegan Fudge Brownies, made with whole wheat flour and wholesome ingredients. The combination of cocoa, walnuts, and optional chocolate chips provides a delightful burst of flavor and texture. Perfect for any occasion, these brownies are sure to impress even the most discerning palates. Enjoy the guilt-free pleasure of these decadent treats!

INGREDIENTS

¼ cup silken tofu, firm tofu, or thick cashew cream

¾ cup chocolate chips (or finely chopped non-dairy cooking chocolate) (optional)

¼ cup chopped walnuts

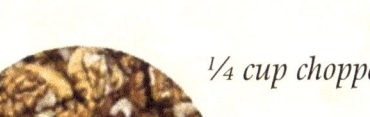

cup cocoa powder

1 tbsp pure vanilla extract

1 ¼ cups date paste

⅓ cup soy milk, plus extra if needed for mixing

½ tsp baking soda

½ tsp unrefined salt

1 tsp baking powder

1 cup whole wheat flour

Golden Vegan Banana Muffins

Method:

1. Begin by mashing the ripe bananas in a bowl, then incorporate 1 tablespoon of citrus juice into the mixture. Set it aside.

2. In a separate bowl, combine the whole wheat flour, salt, and ½ teaspoon of baking soda. Sift the flour to ensure a smooth texture, reserving the remaining ½ teaspoon of baking soda for later use.

3. Utilizing a blender, blend the soy milk and jaggery for approximately 2 minutes until well combined. Gradually add the dry mixture to the blender while it is still running, alternating with the mashed bananas. If the mixture appears slightly dry, add small amounts of soy milk until a smooth consistency is achieved, being cautious not to make it overly runny.

4. Finally, gently fold in 1 tablespoon of citrus juice and ½ teaspoon of baking powder using a spoon. Avoid over-mixing the batter. Pour the mixture into paper cups, filling them up to three-quarters of their height.

5. Preheat the oven to 375 °F (180 °C).

6. Bake the muffins for approximately 20 minutes. To check if they are ready, insert a toothpick into a muffin. If it comes out clean, they are perfectly baked.

Indulge in these delectable Golden Banana Muffins, a delightful treat that combines the natural sweetness of ripe bananas with the wholesome goodness of whole wheat flour, soy milk, and organic jaggery. Enjoy their fluffy texture and delicate citrus undertones as they captivate your taste buds with their simple yet elegant flavors. Perfect for any occasion or as a delightful accompaniment to your favorite warm beverage.

INGREDIENTS

1 cup of soy milk

1 teaspoon of baking soda

2 tablespoons of lemon juice or orange juice

¾ cup of organic jaggery

4 ripe bananas

½ teaspoon of unrefined salt

2 cups of whole wheat flour

Silken Chocolate Delight

Method:

1. Begin by gathering all the necessary ingredients and ensuring they are measured accurately.
2. Peel and pit the ripe avocados, discarding any brown or bruised areas.
3. In a food processor or blender, combine the avocados, unsweetened cocoa powder, and date paste.
4. Blend the ingredients until a smooth and homogeneous mixture is achieved. Ensure that all the ingredients are well incorporated.
5. Transfer the chocolate mousse mixture into small serving bowls or ramekins, distributing it evenly.
6. Place the bowls or ramekins in the refrigerator and allow the mousse to chill for a minimum of 2 hours. This will enhance the texture and flavor.
7. Once the chocolate mousse has set, it is ready to be served and enjoyed. Variation:

If avocados are not readily available, a suitable alternative can be used. Consider substituting 200 g of soaked cashew nuts, tofu, or tender coconut flesh in place of the avocados. These alternatives will provide a creamy texture and complement the rich chocolate flavor of the mousse.
Note: The Silken Chocolate Delight is best enjoyed chilled, and any leftovers can be stored in an airtight container in the refrigerator for up to two days.

INGREDIENTS

½ cup unsweetened cocoa powder

2 ripe avocados

Cocoa-Hazelnut Spread

Method:

1. Preheat the oven to 200°C (392°F).
2. Spread the hazelnuts evenly on a baking sheet and roast them in the preheated oven for 8-10 minutes. The hazelnuts should become glossy and release their natural oils.
3. Allow the roasted hazelnuts to cool until they are slightly warm to the touch.
4. Transfer the hazelnuts to a grinder jar and grind them, making sure to scrape down the sides of the jar periodically. Continue grinding until a smooth butter-like consistency is achieved.
5. Add the pitted soft dates and cacao powder to the hazelnut butter in the grinder jar. Grind the mixture into a velvety paste, ensuring to scrape down the sides of the jar as needed. Do not add water during this process.
6. Transfer the vegan Nutella into an airtight jar for storage. Serving size: 10-12

Indulge in the luscious flavors of our exquisite Cocoa-Hazelnut Spread, a delectable vegan alternative to the beloved classic. The harmonious combination of roasted hazelnuts, tender pitted dates, and organic cacao powder creates a silky smooth texture that will delight your taste buds. Perfect as a spread on toast, a dip for fresh fruits, or a heavenly ingredient in your favorite recipes. Prepare to savor the ultimate in vegan indulgence with every spoonful.

INGREDIENTS

1 cup pitted soft dates

¼ cup organic cacao powder

½ cup premium quality hazelnuts

Creamy Green Delight: Avocado and Miso Dip

Method:

1. Begin by mashing the avocado until it reaches a smooth consistency.
2. Add the miso paste, finely minced garlic, finely chopped onion, lemon juice, grated red radishes, and mustard to the mashed avocado.
3. Mix all the ingredients thoroughly until well combined.
4. Taste the dip and adjust the seasoning with unrefined salt if necessary, keeping in mind that miso paste already contributes to saltiness.
5. Serve the Avocado and Miso Dip as a spread on bread or as a dip alongside freshly sliced vegetables.
6. This recipe yields approximately four servings.

Enjoy the luscious and flavorful Creamy Green Delight, perfect for elegant gatherings or sophisticated snacking.

INGREDIENTS

½ teaspoon mustard

1 large or two small red radishes, finely grated

¼ of an onion, finely chopped

Unrefined salt to taste (if needed, as the miso paste is already salty)

1 teaspoon lemon juice

1 clove garlic, finely minced

1 large ripe avocado

1 teaspoon miso paste

Eggplant Elegance: Refined Aubergine Delicacy

Method:

1. Preheat the oven to 375 °F (190 °C).
2. Begin by making several cuts on the aubergines and carefully insert the slivered garlic into the cuts.
3. Place the prepared aubergines on a baking sheet lined with parchment paper and bake them until they become soft, which should take approximately 40 minutes.
4. Allow the baked aubergines to cool, and then remove the skin.
5. Transfer the skinned aubergines to a blender, along with the tahini paste, lemon juice, and unrefined salt.
6. Process the ingredients in the blender until they achieve a smooth consistency.
7. Serve the Aubergine Caviar at room temperature to fully appreciate its flavors.

Yield: This exquisite dish serves 8-10, making it ideal for gatherings or sophisticated occasions.

INGREDIENTS

Juice of 1 lemon

1/2 teaspoon of unrefined salt, or to taste

2 large cloves of garlic, slivered

1/2 cup of tahini paste (sesame butter)

1 large or 2 medium aubergines (bharta baingan)

Savory Tofu Delight: Exquisite Sandwich Spread

Method:

1. Begin by gently crumbling the premium tofu into a mixing bowl, ensuring a consistent texture throughout.
2. Add the finely chopped onion, tomatoes, and capsicum to the bowl, combining them with the crumbled tofu.
3. Season the mixture with unrefined salt and freshly ground black pepper, adjusting the quantities to suit your preferred taste profile.
4. Introduce ground mustard to the blend, adding a delightful touch of piquancy. Adjust the quantity based on personal preference.
5. Sprinkle in the finely chopped green coriander leaves, infusing the spread with a fresh and aromatic element.
6. For those seeking an added kick, consider incorporating a small amount of finely chopped green chillies to lend a subtle heat to the spread. Note that this step is optional and can be skipped for milder palates.

7. Thoroughly mix all the ingredients, ensuring they are evenly distributed and well combined.
8. Once prepared, this sublime tofu sandwich spread is ready to grace your culinary creations. Serve it generously on your favorite choice of bread or sandwich base, elevating your meal with its luscious texture and flavors.

Yield: This delectable tofu spread recipe yields approximately 8 to 10 servings, allowing for ample enjoyment and sharing.
Indulge in the sophisticated and flavorful experience provided by Savory Tofu Delight: Exquisite Sandwich Spread, guaranteed to add a touch of class to any culinary affair.

INGREDIENTS

(200 g) of premium tofu

⅛ tsp of finely chopped green chillies (optional)

1 medium-sized onion, finely chopped

¼ cup of finely chopped capsicum

2 small tomatoes, finely chopped

A handful of fresh green coriander leaves, finely chopped

Unrefined salt and freshly ground black pepper, to taste

Ground mustard, to taste

Delicate Cashew Medley: A Refined Vegan Sandwich Spread

Method:

1. In a high-speed blender, combine all the ingredients, except for the parsley, celery, and white onion.
2. Blend the mixture until it reaches a smooth and creamy consistency.
3. Gradually incorporate the finely chopped parsley, celery, and white onion into the blended mixture.
4. Stir gently until all the ingredients are well combined.
5. Congratulations! You have now prepared an exquisite, wholesome raw sandwich spread, reminiscent of a delectable mayonnaise.

Note: This vegan sandwich spread is best enjoyed chilled and can be stored in an airtight container in the refrigerator for up to five days.

INGREDIENTS

Unrefined salt, to taste

1 tomato, chopped

2 tablespoons freshly squeezed lemon juice

2 cups raw cashew nuts

1 red capsicum, minced

1 clove of garlic, finely chopped

2 stalks celery, finely chopped

½ white onion, chopped

2 teaspoons finely chopped parsley

Savory Lentil Medley Bread

Method:

1. Begin by thoroughly washing both the split black gram and split green gram dals. Then, soak them separately in water for approximately 4 to 5 hours.
2. After the soaking time, rinse and drain the soaked dals.
3. Grind the split black gram and split green gram dals separately until you achieve a smooth batter-like consistency.
4. Combine both dal batters in a mixing bowl and add a suitable amount of unrefined salt to taste. Gently stir the mixture until well incorporated.
5. Set the batter aside in a warm place for approximately 7 to 8 hours, allowing it to ferment. This fermentation process enhances the flavors and texture of the bread.
6. Once the fermentation is complete, prepare a steamer for cooking. Pour the batter into a greased steaming dish or mold.
7. Steam the batter for about 5 to 10 minutes, or until the bread is cooked through and firm to the touch.

8. Once steamed, allow the bread to cool down before slicing it into desired portions.
9. Serve the Lentil Medley Bread by spreading a layer of flavorful green chutney or peanut butter on each slice.
10. For an extra touch of freshness and appeal, garnish with thinly sliced cucumber, tomato, or any other preferred toppings.
11. Enjoy the delightful flavors and wholesome goodness of this Savory Lentil Medley Bread as a nutritious snack or part of a balanced meal.

Note: This bread can be stored in an airtight container for a few days, but it is best consumed fresh for optimal taste and texture.

INGREDIENTS

1 cup split green gram (mung dal)

1 cup split black gram (urad dal)

Unrefined salt

Sophisticated Gluten-Free Pizza Canvas

Method:

1. In a mixing bowl, combine the gluten-free flour, coconut or cashew butter, powdered dried herbs, and unrefined salt. Mix well until you achieve a crumbly texture.
2. Gradually add one tablespoon of warm water at a time to the mixture. Knead the ingredients together until a soft dough forms.
3. Divide the dough into two equal-sized balls.
4. Dust a clean surface with flour and gently press one of the dough balls using your fingertips. Aim for a thicker center and thinner edges, shaping it into a 6-inch wide disc.
5. Heat a tawa (griddle) and place the dough disc on it. Roast the dough until it reaches about 60% doneness.
6. Your gluten-free pizza base is now ready!

To Assemble the Pizza:

1. Preheat your oven to 180 °C.
2. Take the prepared pizza base and spread a layer of pizza sauce over it.
3. Add your choice of cashew cheese and vegetables as desired.
4. Place the pizza in the preheated oven and bake for approximately 20-25 minutes or until the cheese on top turns golden brown.

Indulge in the delectable flavors of this Sophisticated Gluten-Free Pizza Canvas, a gluten-free delight that will satisfy your cravings while accommodating dietary restrictions.

INGREDIENTS

2-3 tablespoons of coconut or cashew butter

1 teaspoon of unrefined salt

¼ to ½ cup of warm water

1 cup of gluten-free flour
(choose from options such as buckwheat, amaranth, or sorghum)

1 teaspoon of powdered dried herbs
(a blend of oregano, basil, and thyme)

Gourmet Whole Wheat Pancakes

Method:

1. In a mixing bowl, combine the whole wheat flour, baking soda, and baking powder.
2. Add the date paste and soy milk (or water) to the dry ingredients. Stir until well combined. If the batter appears too thick, gradually add 1 tablespoon of water at a time until reaching the desired consistency.
3. Heat a non-stick pan over medium heat.
4. Pour a ladleful of the pancake batter onto the hot pan, spreading it slightly to form a round shape. Cook until the edges begin to brown and bubbles appear on the surface of the pancake.
5. Carefully flip the pancake with a spatula and cook the other side until golden brown.
6. Repeat the process with the remaining batter, adjusting the heat as needed to prevent burning.
7. Serve the pancakes hot and enjoy!

Note: These Gourmet Whole Wheat Pancakes are fluffy, nutritious, and have a delightful hint of sweetness from the date paste. They make a perfect breakfast or brunch option for those seeking a healthier alternative to traditional pancakes.

INGREDIENTS

1½ cups whole wheat flour

1 tablespoon date paste

1½ cups soy milk or water

½ teaspoon baking soda

1 teaspoon baking powder

Whole Wheat Baguette Delight

Method:

1. In a mixing bowl, whisk together soy milk, whole wheat flour, nutritional yeast, date paste, and ground cinnamon until well combined.
2. Place the bread slices in a shallow dish and pour the mixture over them, ensuring each slice is thoroughly coated. Allow the bread to soak in the mixture until it softens.
3. Heat a skillet over medium heat and lightly grease it.
4. Cook each bread slice on the skillet until both sides turn golden brown and crispy, which should take about 5-7 minutes per slice.
5. Once cooked, remove the French toast from the skillet and serve it warm with the delectable syrup (recipe below).

For the Syrup

Method:

1. In a saucepan, combine ⅔ cup of juice, chopped strawberries, and ground cinnamon. Bring the mixture to a boil over medium heat.
2. Reduce the heat and let the mixture simmer for 5 minutes, allowing the flavors to meld together.
3. In a separate bowl, add the date paste to the remaining juice and stir until well combined.
4. Pour the date paste mixture into the simmering strawberry mixture and continue to simmer, stirring occasionally, until the juices thicken to a desired consistency.
5. Once the syrup has thickened, remove it from the heat and serve it hot over the French toast, adding an extra touch of indulgence.

Enjoy the exquisite Whole Wheat Baguette Delight, featuring delightfully crispy French toast complemented by the luscious and flavorsome syrup. This sophisticated and health-conscious breakfast option is sure to please your palate and elevate your mornings to new levels of culinary bliss.

INGREDIENTS

2 tablespoons nutritional yeast

8-12 thick slices of whole wheat bread or baguette

2 teaspoons date paste

¼ cup whole wheat flour

3 cups soy milk

2 teaspoons ground cinnamon

Golden Garbanzo Brunch Delights

Method:

1. Preheat a regular waffle iron (not Belgian) to the desired baking temperature.
2. In a blender, combine the whole-grain cornmeal (or alternative flour), garbanzo beans, salt, vanilla extract, date paste, water, and rolled oats.
3. Blend the ingredients until smooth, approximately 30 seconds, or until a well-blended batter is achieved.
4. Pour the batter into the preheated waffle iron, filling the molds evenly.
5. Close the waffle iron and bake at medium setting until the waffle iron signals that the baking process is complete. The baking time may vary depending on the specific waffle iron used. For instance, a Cuisinart Classic Round Waffle Maker, typically takes under 3 minutes, while other waffle irons may require 8-10 minutes.
6. Once the waffle is cooked to perfection, carefully remove it from the waffle iron and place it on a serving plate.
7. Serve the elevated grain and bean waffles warm, accompanied by your favorite toppings such as fresh fruits, whipped cream, or maple syrup.

Enjoy the exquisite flavors and delightful textures of these refined Golden Garbanzo Brunch Delights, perfect for a sophisticated breakfast or brunch experience.

INGREDIENTS

½ teaspoon of salt

½ can of garbanzo beans, rinsed and drained, or ½ cup of boiled garbanzo beans

¼ cup of whole grain cornmeal (or ¼ cup of millet, quinoa, or buckwheat flour)

1 ¾ cups of water

1 tablespoon of date paste

1 tablespoon of vanilla extract

2 cups of rolled oats

Vegan Tofu Cinnamon French Toast with Date Infusion

Method:

1. In a blender, combine the tofu, water, date paste, cinnamon powder, and ripe banana. Blend until the mixture is smooth and well incorporated.
2. Pour the tofu mixture into a shallow dish, creating a smooth and even layer.
3. Dip each slice of whole wheat bread into the tofu mixture, ensuring that both sides are coated thoroughly.
4. Heat a non-stick pan over medium heat or preheat an oven to 200 °C (392 °F).
5. If using a pan, place the coated bread slices onto the hot pan and cook for about 2-3 minutes on each side until golden brown. If using an oven, arrange the coated bread slices on a baking sheet and bake for approximately 5 minutes, turning them over once the edges begin to brown.
6. Once cooked, remove the French toast from the heat source and transfer it to serving plates.
7. Garnish with fresh berries or drizzle with a luscious date syrup to enhance the flavors.

8. Serve the Vegan Tofu Cinnamon French Toast immediately, while still warm, to fully enjoy its delightful texture and taste.

__Enjoy this delectable and nutritious breakfast option that seamlessly combines the smoothness of tofu with the comforting essence of cinnamon, creating a memorable dining experience.__

INGREDIENTS

250 g tofu

½ tsp cinnamon powder

½ cup water

1 tsp date paste

GOLDEN TOFU MEDLEY

Method:

1. Begin by draining the tofu and carefully crumbling it into small pieces.
2. Heat a sauté pan over medium heat and add the minced garlic, onions, and diced red bell pepper. Sauté the mixture without oil for approximately 2 minutes, until the vegetables become fragrant and slightly tender.
3. Incorporate the chopped mushrooms into the pan and continue stirring.
4. Add the crumbled tofu to the pan, followed by the turmeric powder, salt, and freshly ground black pepper. Thoroughly combine all the ingredients, ensuring that the tofu is evenly coated with the spices.
5. Turn off the heat and garnish the tofu scramble with freshly chopped parsley for a vibrant touch.
6. Serve the delectable Golden Tofu Medley, a harmonious fusion of flavors and textures that is sure to delight the palate.

Enjoy this elegant and flavorful plant-based dish as a wholesome breakfast or a delightful addition to any meal.

INGREDIENTS

300 g firm tofu

cup minced onion

½ tsp turmeric powder (haldi)

3 cloves garlic, peeled and minced (1½ tbsp)

1 tbsp freshly chopped parsley

½ cup chopped mushrooms

½ tsp unrefined salt

3 tbsp diced red bell pepper

¼ tsp freshly ground black pepper

Delicate Herb-Infused Potato Galettes

Method:

1. Begin by placing the grated potatoes in a colander and position it over a large bowl. Gently squeeze the potatoes with your hands to remove any excess liquid. Discard the liquid and transfer the potatoes to the bowl.

2. Add the grated yellow onion, minced fresh parsley, whole wheat flour, baking powder, salt, and freshly ground black pepper to the bowl with the potatoes. Thoroughly mix all the ingredients until well combined.

3. Preheat a large skillet over medium heat. Scoop a heaped tablespoon of the batter onto the skillet and flatten it to form a pancake. Repeat this process to create three or four more potato pancakes, ensuring they are not overcrowded in the skillet.

4. Cook the potato pancakes for approximately 8 minutes, flipping them once, until both sides are golden brown.

5. Repeat the cooking process with the remaining potato mixture until all the pancakes are cooked. Transfer the cooked potato pancakes to a baking tray, and then place them in an oven to keep them warm until serving time.
6. When ready to serve, present the delectable potato galettes alongside a side of ketchup or vegan sour cream, allowing your guests to enhance their flavors as desired.

Enjoy these exquisite Herb-infused Potato Galettes, perfect for a sophisticated vegan dining experience.

INGREDIENTS

1 tablespoon fresh parsley, minced

1 teaspoon unrefined salt

1/4 cup whole wheat flour

700 g potatoes, grated with peel on

1/4 teaspoon freshly ground black pepper

1 small yellow onion, grated

1/2 teaspoon baking powder

Creamy Avocado Sunrise Bowl

Method:

1. In a blender, combine the ripe avocado, red banana, strawberries, and pitted dates. Blend until smooth and achieve a creamy, yogurt-like consistency.
2. Transfer the blended mixture to a cereal bowl.
3. Garnish the avocado mixture with a generous topping of frozen berries, chopped nuts, and seeds.
4. Serve and enjoy this delightful Creamy Avocado Sunrise Bowl.

Variation:

For a luscious chocolate smoothie bowl:

- Add 1-2 tbsp of raw cacao powder to the blender.
- Increase the quantity of bananas and dates.
- Follow the same instructions as above.

INGREDIENTS

4-5 tbsp frozen mixed berries
(strawberries, figs, raisins, or any other berries of choice)

2 pitted dates
(for enhanced sweetness)

½ ripe avocado, peeled and pitted

1-2 tbsp chopped nuts and seeds

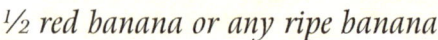

½ red banana or any ripe banana

Gourmet Delight Wrap

Method:

1. Preheat a griddle (tawa) over medium heat.
2. Place the whole wheat base on the griddle and heat until lightly roasted on both sides.
3. Once the base is roasted, spread the preferred spread evenly over the surface, leaving a border around the edges.
4. Arrange the grilled or raw vegetables on top of the spread, distributing them evenly across the base.
5. If desired, add any optional spikes or additions, such as chilli sauce, onions, mustard, marinated tofu, or beans.
6. Carefully roll the wrap tightly, starting from one end, until it forms a compact roll, similar to a Frankie.
7. Serve the Gourmet Delight Wrap immediately while it is still warm.

Enjoy the delightful combination of flavors and textures in this elegantly prepared Gourmet Delight Wrap.

INGREDIENTS

Optional additions: marinated or grilled tofu, beans, etc.

Assorted grilled or raw vegetables of your choice

1 large whole wheat base (tortilla/chapatis, etc.), with or without flavoring (tomato, spinach, etc.)

Optional spikes: chilli sauce, onions, mustard, etc.

Basil-Infused Tomato Bruschetta with Homemade Pesto

Method:

1. Prepare the pesto by combining the pine nuts, garlic, fresh basil leaves, unrefined salt, lemon juice, and water in a food processor. Blend until smooth and creamy. Transfer the pesto to a bowl and set it aside.

2. In a separate bowl, mix together the chopped tomatoes, minced garlic, fresh basil leaves, balsamic vinegar, and unrefined salt. Combine well to ensure all the flavors are evenly distributed. Set the topping aside.

3. Toast the slices of whole wheat bread until they turn golden and crispy.

4. Once the bread slices are toasted, spread a generous amount of the homemade pesto on each slice.

5. Next, spoon the tomato topping mixture evenly over the pesto-covered bread slices. Ensure that the topping is spread out to cover the entire surface.

6. For an elegant touch, garnish each bruschetta with black olive rings and fresh whole basil leaves.

7. Serve the tomato bruschetta with pesto immediately, allowing the flavors to meld together while the bread is still warm and crispy.

Enjoy this exquisite Basil-infused Tomato Bruschetta with Homemade Pesto as an appetizer or light meal.

INGREDIENTS

⅛ tsp of unrefined salt

2 tbsp of balsamic vinegar

4 tomatoes, chopped

⅓ cup of pine nuts, cashew nuts, or walnuts

2 cloves of garlic

1 tbsp of lemon

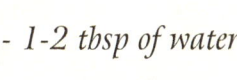

- 1-2 tbsp of water

1 clove of garlic

10 fresh basil leaves

Gourmet Plant-Based Burger

Method:

1. In a large skillet, sauté the diced onion and bell pepper over medium heat for 2 to 3 minutes, or until the onions are soft and translucent.
2. Reduce the heat to medium-low and add the vegetable stock, tomato sauce, chilli powder, soy sauce, date paste, soy granules, and a pinch of unrefined salt and pepper. Stir well to combine all the ingredients.
3. If desired, add a dash of hot sauce or Tabasco sauce to enhance the spiciness of the burger mixture.
4. Allow the mixture to simmer for at least 15 minutes, ensuring that the soy granules absorb the flavors and soften.
5. Toast the whole wheat hamburger buns lightly to add a crunchy texture.
6. Spoon the flavorful vegan burger mixture onto the buns and spread it evenly.
7. Serve the Gourmet Plant-Based Burgers hot, accompanied by your preferred condiments, providing a delightful culinary experience.

Yield: This recipe serves 5-6 individuals, making it ideal for a gathering or a family meal.

INGREDIENTS

1 diced green or red bell pepper

1 diced onion

1 tablespoon date paste

1 tablespoon chilli powder

1 tablespoon soy sauce

1½ cups vegetable stock

5-6 whole wheat hamburger buns

Unrefined salt and pepper to taste

Dash of hot sauce or Tabasco sauce (optional)

Whole Wheat Blueberry Pancakes

Method:

1. In separate bowls, prepare the wet and dry ingredients.
2. In the wet ingredient bowl, pour the soy milk and gently whisk it.
3. In the dry ingredient bowl, combine the whole wheat flour, blueberries, baking powder, and unrefined salt. Mix them evenly.
4. Gradually add the dry ingredient mixture to the wet ingredients. Stir gently until the ingredients are just combined, making sure not to overmix the batter.
5. Heat a pan over medium heat until hot.
6. Pour a ladleful of the batter onto the hot pan. Cook the pancake until the edges start to appear dry.
7. Carefully flip the pancake and continue cooking until it is thoroughly done and golden brown on both sides.
8. Repeat the process with the remaining batter, cooking each pancake one at a time.
9. Serve the whole wheat blueberry pancakes hot, and enjoy their delightful flavor.

Note: You may garnish the pancakes with additional blueberries and a drizzle of maple syrup for an extra touch of elegance.

INGREDIENTS

1 ¼ cups whole wheat flour

2 teaspoons baking powder

½ teaspoon unrefined salt

½ cup soy milk

⅓ cup blueberries

Gourmet Herb-Roasted Potato Wedges

Method:

1. Begin by steaming the potato wedges until they are approximately 70% cooked.
2. Preheat the oven to 180 °C-200 °C.
3. In a mixing bowl, combine the coconut milk with the dry mixed herbs and salt. Stir well to create a flavorful herb-infused mixture.
4. Add the potato wedges to the bowl and toss them gently, ensuring that each wedge is thoroughly coated with the herb mixture.
5. Line a baking tray with parchment paper and arrange the coated wedges in a single layer.
6. Place the tray in the preheated oven and bake for 15-20 minutes, or until the wedges turn golden and crisp.
7. Carefully flip the wedges over using tongs or a spatula, and continue baking for an additional 5-10 minutes to achieve optimal crispness and tenderness.
8. Once the potato wedges are golden and cooked to perfection, remove them from the oven.
9. Serve these delectable herb-roasted potato wedges alongside a choice of homemade ketchup or green chutney for an extra burst of flavor.

Indulge in the elegant and savory delight of our Gourmet Herb-Roasted Potato Wedges, the perfect accompaniment to any meal.

INGREDIENTS

4 medium unpeeled sweet potatoes/potatoes, thoroughly rinsed and cut into wedges

4 tablespoons coconut milk

1-2 teaspoons of dry mixed herbs, such as parsley, thyme, rosemary, cayenne, etc.

¼ teaspoon unrefined salt

Nutty Date Granola Bars

Method:

1. Preheat the oven to 180°C (350°F).
2. Spread the rolled oats and chopped almonds on a baking sheet and toast them in the preheated oven for 13-15 minutes or until they turn a slightly golden brown color.
3. In a food processor, process the dates until they form small bits, creating a dough-like consistency, which should take approximately 1 minute.
4. In a large mixing bowl, combine the toasted oats, almonds, chopped dates, chia seeds, sunflower seeds, flax seeds, and hemp seeds.
5. In a small saucepan, warm the date paste, coconut butter, and creamy salted natural peanut butter or almond butter over low heat. Stir the mixture until well combined.
6. Pour the warm mixture over the oats and nuts in the mixing bowl. Mix thoroughly, breaking up the dates to ensure even distribution throughout the mixture. You can use a spoon or your hands for this step.
7. Line an 8" x 8" dish or any other small pan with parchment paper, allowing for easy removal of the granola bars later.

8. Transfer the mixture to the lined dish and cover it with another piece of parchment paper. Press down firmly on the mixture using a flat object, such as a book, to pack it tightly. This will help prevent the bars from becoming crumbly.
9. Place the dish in the refrigerator or freezer for 15-20 minutes to allow the bars to harden.
10. Once firm, remove the slab from the dish and neatly cut it into 10 even bars.
11. Store the granola bars in an airtight container in the refrigerator for up to a few days.

Enjoy the delightful and nutritious Nutty Date Granola Bars at any time of the day!

INGREDIENTS

½ cup raw almonds, walnuts, or pecans, roughly chopped

¼ cup date paste

2 tbsp coconut butter

1½ cups rolled oats

1 cup tightly packed pitted dates

2 tbsp chia seeds

2 tbsp sunflower seeds (roasted or raw)

2 tbsp hemp seeds

¼ cup creamy salted natural peanut butter or almond butter

2 tbsp flax seeds (ground or whole)

71

Roasted Sweet Potato Delight

Method:

1. Preheat the oven to 180 °C. If using sweet potatoes, wash them well and chop them into 1-inch cubes with the skin on. Steam the cubes for 5-6 minutes.

   If using purple yam (kand), wash it, remove the skin, cut it into pieces, and steam it for 5-6 minutes.

2. Place the steamed sweet potatoes or purple yam in a baking dish and pour the coconut milk over them. Bake until they turn golden.

3. Add the crushed peanuts, finely chopped coriander leaves, roasted cumin powder, spicy green chutney, red chilli powder, finely chopped green chillies, black salt, unrefined salt, black pepper powder, and coriander powder to the baked sweet potatoes or purple yam. Mix well to combine.

4. Adjust the taste by adding more spice, tamarind paste, or lemon juice according to your preference.

5. Garnish with fresh mint leaves and serve the Roasted Sweet Potato Delight.

Note: This recipe can be customized to suit your taste by adjusting the seasoning and spiciness levels. Enjoy the delightful combination of roasted sweet potatoes or purple yam with the flavors of coconut, peanuts, and spices.

INGREDIENTS

1-2 tablespoons spicy green chutney, to taste

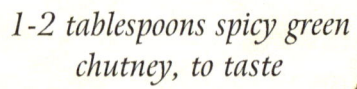

500 g unpeeled sweet potatoes or purple yam (kand)

1 1/2 teaspoons finely chopped green chillies

1 teaspoon red chilli powder

1/4 cup finely chopped fresh coriander leaves

1/2 teaspoon roasted cumin (jeera) powder

1/2 cup thick coconut milk

1/2 teaspoon black salt (kala namak)

1/2 cup roasted unpeeled peanuts, coarsely crushed

1 teaspoon unrefined salt (sendha namak)

www.ingramcontent.com/pod-product-compliance
Lightning Source LLC
LaVergne TN
LVHW070523070526
838199LV00072B/6687